Bye Bye Ja

by Simon Ad

THE CAST

MOUSE

BEN

JOJO

RAVI

BILLY

SAM

MRS GOHILL
Ravi's mother

MRS STEEL
Billy's mother

TARA GOHILL
Ravi's cousin, aged 3

JASMINE STEEL
Billy's little sister, aged 1

MRS AMBROSE
the children's class teacher

MR GREEN
a neighbour

Scene 1

Classroom in Story Street School at the end of the school day. Mrs Ambrose is seeing the children out of the room.

MRS AMBROSE Mind how you go, Ben. Don't forget your lunchbox, Duncan. Mouse?

MOUSE Yes, miss?

MRS AMBROSE You haven't forgotten your reading book, have you?

MOUSE Whoops. I'll just go and get it.

Mouse rushes off.

MRS AMBROSE Ah, Billy. I've got a message for you from Mrs Ray in the school office.

BILLY Yes, miss.
Billy, Ravi and Sam come over.

MRS AMBROSE It's from your mum. You and Ravi are to go straight to Tadpoles and meet your mothers there.

SAM Tadpoles?

BILLY That's the nursery where my sister Jasmine goes.

SAM Sounds more like a swimming club.

BILLY Mum's helping out today. So's Ravi's mum, because his cousin Tara goes there as well.

SAM So why have you got to go up there?

BILLY I expect Mum's got to stay on a bit to help clear up.

RAVI You should see the mess those toddlers make. It looks like a bomb's hit the place by the end of the day. And then they have to disinfect all the cars and the building bricks.

SAM Why?

RAVI You don't want to know.

BILLY   Why don't you come up with us and see for yourself, Sam?

SAM   Er … I'm not sure.

BILLY   Go on, it's a great laugh. We can mess around in their playground, and they always give us biscuits and a drink.

RAVI   And there are always a few little ones we have to look after while the grown-ups tidy up. It's good fun.

SAM   Oh, all right. Just for half an hour. I need to be back when Mum comes in from work.

BILLY   Great! Let's go. Bye, Mrs Ambrose.

MRS AMBROSE Bye, Billy. Bye, Ravi. Bye, Sam. See you tomorrow.

Exit Billy, Ravi and Sam.

Scene 2

At the nursery. Mrs Steel and Mrs Gohill are wiping down table tops. Jasmine and Tara are playing in a corner with a pile of toys.

Enter Billy, Ravi and Sam.

MRS STEEL	Well done, boys, you got my message.
BILLY	Yes, Mum, and Sam's come with us.
MRS GOHILL	Hello, Sam.
SAM	Hello, Mrs Gohill.
MRS STEEL	Does your mum know you're here, Sam?
SAM	It'll be all right as long as I'm home by 4.30.

MRS STEEL	We'll only be a little while and then we'll all walk back together. Maybe we'll get an ice cream on the way.
SAM	Thanks, Mrs Steel. That would be great.
MRS GOHILL	Did you have a good day at school, Ravi?
RAVI	Yes, Mum.
MRS GOHILL	What did you do in class?
RAVI	Nothing much.
MRS GOHILL	I want you three to look after Jasmine and Tara in here. Billy's mum and I are going outside to tidy up the play equipment.
BILLY	Fine.

MRS STEEL	You won't forget to keep an eye on the little ones, will you?
BILLY	No, Mum.
MRS STEEL	Sure?
BILLY	We'll be fine, Mum. *(To Jasmine and Tara)* Hey, girls, are you going to come and play with us? *Jasmine and Tara run over. They are very excited.*
TARA	Yeah!
RAVI	What do you want to play?
TARA	Firefighters. *Tara gets a firefighter's helmet from the dressing-up box.*

MRS STEEL   Don't you go getting them overexcited.

MRS GOHILL   Call us if you need us.

Exit Mrs Steel and Mrs Gohill.

TARA   *(Jumping up and down)* Firefighters! Firefighters!

JASMINE   *(Trying to copy Tara)* Farmer! Farmer!

SAM   What will we use for a fire engine?

TARA   Billy! Billy be a fire engine.

BILLY   OK. Give us a push, Sam.
Sam pushes Billy around the room in his wheelchair. Billy makes siren noises and Sam makes engine noises. Jasmine and Tara toddle after them looking excited.

9

BILLY	Nee-nar! Nee-nar!
JASMINE	Fire! Fire!
TARA	Billy go faster.
JASMINE	Billy fast. *Sam pushes Billy faster and the chair crashes into a big piece of play equipment.*
SAM	Whoops!
JASMINE	Billy crash! Billy crash!
TARA	Oh dear! All broken!
BILLY	She's right – it is a bit broken. What shall we do?

RAVI	Try and fix it. *(He bends over to look at the damage.)* It's only a little bit broken. I'm sure no one will notice. Just push it back together. What do you think?
SAM	Hmm. You can still see where it's cracked. *Jasmine is running around making crashing noises.*
JASMINE	Billy crash! Bang!
BILLY	Be quiet, Jasmine.
JASMINE	Crash! Jaffim crash!

BILLY   *(Cross)* Just leave us alone, will you. Buzz off!
Jasmine runs off.

BILLY   Why don't we turn it round, so the cracked bit is at the back. Then no one will know.
They turn the play equipment round.

TARA   More fire engine?

RAVI   Not now, Tara.

TARA   Please, Billy. One more fire engine.

RAVI   I think we'd better play something else now. Oh, look, here comes Mum.

Enter Mrs Gohill and Mrs Steel.

MRS GOHILL   What a lot of noise you've been making in here. What have you all been up to?

BILLY   *(Quickly)* We were just messing around with the little ones and we got a little game going for them.

TARA   And Jaffim bye-bye.

MRS STEEL   That's a point. Where is Jasmine?

TARA   Jaffim bye-bye.

MRS STEEL   *(Worried)* Tara, do you know where Jasmine is?

TARA   Yes.

MRS STEEL   Tell us, darling, where is Jasmine?

TARA   Jaffim bye-bye.

13

MRS STEEL	Didn't any of you see her go? *Long pause. Sam, Billy and Ravi say nothing.*
MRS STEEL	Well?
BILLY	I'm sorry, Mum. I really am. We got into the game and we just didn't notice her slip out.
MRS STEEL	*(Angry)* Honestly. All I ask you to do is keep an eye on them and you can't even do that properly. You've really let me down.
SAM	We're very sorry, Mrs Steel.

MRS STEEL   Well, you can help us to look for her now. We'll start by searching outside the building and then we'll work our way towards our house. She might have wandered home.

MRS GOHILL   You, Billy and Sam, go that way. I'll take Ravi and Tara and we'll go up to the play park and see if she's there.

MRS STEEL   We'll meet up back at the hall in ten minutes.

They all leave in a hurry. As they go, they are calling Jasmine's name.

MRS GOHILL   Jasmine!

MRS STEEL   Jasmine! Where are you, love? Jasmine!

Scene 3

Outside in the street. Mrs Steel, Billy and Sam are searching. In the distance Mr Green is walking his dog, Scrap.

MRS STEEL   *(Calling)* Jasmine! Jasmine!

BILLY   Look! There's Mr Green walking his dog. Maybe he's seen Jasmine.

SAM   Mr Green! Mr Green!
Mr Green comes up to join them.

MR GREEN   Hello, there, Sam. What's all the fuss about?

SAM   It's Jasmine Steel, Billy's sister.

MR GREEN   Oh yes?

SAM   Have you seen her recently?

MR GREEN   Oh yes.

MRS STEEL   Where was she going? What time was it?

MR GREEN   Let me think now. I think it was yesterday morning, or maybe it was the day before. Now, where was she going? –

MRS STEEL   *(Interrupting)* Oh, this is hopeless. At this rate we'll never find her. Come on, everyone.

MR GREEN   Wait a minute, I haven't told you yet …
Mrs Steel rushes off followed by Sam and Billy.
Mr Green is left alone, looking angry.

MR GREEN   *(Muttering to himself)* I don't know. Some
people are just so rude! Always in a hurry,
no time to be polite. Fussing over nothing.
Come on, Scrap.

At the playground. Jojo, Mouse and Ben are playing.

Ravi rushes up to them, followed by Mrs Gohill and Tara.

RAVI	Mouse, Jojo, Ben! You've got to help us.
BEN	Hi, Ravi. What's up?
RAVI	I'm looking for Jasmine Steel.
MOUSE	Who?
RAVI	You know, Billy's little sister.
TARA	Jaffim bye-bye.

18

RAVI I'm trying to find her and I thought she might have come along here.

JOJO Oh, I get it. You're playing hide-and-seek. Aren't you a bit old to be playing with toddlers?

RAVI Look, this isn't a game. We've lost her.

MOUSE Lost her?

RAVI Billy and I were helping our mums out at the nursery. We were supposed to be looking after the children, only we've lost Jasmine.

MRS GOHILL We thought she might have come up here.

BEN	We haven't seen her, have we?
JOJO	No. When did she go missing?
MRS GOHILL	It can only have been about ten minutes ago. How long have you been down here?
MOUSE	Ben's mum picked us up from school and we came down here straightaway.
JOJO	We've been here for at least half an hour. She hasn't been here.
MRS GOHILL	You're sure about that?
MOUSE	Certain.
MRS GOHILL	We'd better go back to the hall. If you see Jasmine, will you come and tell us?
BEN	Of course we will, Mrs Gohill. Good luck.

Exit Mrs Gohill, Ravi and Tara.

Scene 5

Back at the nursery. Ten minutes later.

Enter Mrs Steel, Billy and Sam.

BILLY What are we going to do now, Mum?

MRS STEEL We'd best wait for Ravi and his mum, in case they've found her down at the park. You know how much Jasmine likes the swings and slides.

BILLY But what if she isn't there?

MRS STEEL We'll ring the police and report it. They're sure to find her.

SAM I'm so sorry, Mrs Steel.

MRS STEEL Don't worry too much, Sam. It'll turn out all right in the end. Ah, here come the others.

Enter Mrs Gohill, Ravi and Tara.

MRS STEEL Any luck?

MRS GOHILL I'm afraid not. No sign of her anywhere. We asked lots of people on the way but no one has seen her.

TARA Jaffim bye-bye.

MRS STEEL	I'm going to call the police now. We mustn't waste any more time. *Mrs Steel picks up the phone and dials.*
MRS STEEL	*(On the phone)* Hello. Police please. Yes. I'm ringing from the Tadpoles Day Nursery in Story Street and I'd like to report a missing child.
TARA	Jaffim bye-bye.
MRS GOHILL	Tara. Leave Mrs Steel alone, there's a good girl. She's busy. Come and play over here.
MRS STEEL	*(On the phone)* My name is Mrs Wendy Steel. The missing child is my daughter, Jasmine Steel.
TARA	*(Pointing towards the home corner)* Look. Jaffim bye-bye.
MRS STEEL	*(On the phone)* One year old. Fair hair. Wearing a bright red T-shirt and white shorts.
TARA	Look. Jaffim bye-bye. *Tara is pointing to the home corner. Jasmine is fast asleep, curled up on a bean bag under a counter. Ravi, Sam, Billy and Mrs Gohill gather round.*
SAM	So that's where she's been!

BILLY   Mum! Over here! It's all right. We've found her.

MRS STEEL *(On the phone)* I'm very sorry, Officer, it looks like we've made a big mistake.
Mrs Steel puts the phone down and rushes over to join the others.

MRS STEEL Oh, thank goodness you've found her. Well done, Tara.

TARA   Shhh. Jaffim bye-bye. Jaffim gone sleepybyes.

MRS GOHILL   Tara, did you know that Jasmine was sleeping?

TARA   Mmm. Jaffim bye-bye.

MRS GOHILL   But why didn't you tell us?

RAVI   (*Laughing*) She told us lots of times. We just didn't understand what she meant when she kept saying, "Jaffim bye-bye."

MRS STEEL   Never mind now. Let's just be glad she's safe and sound. To think that the little monkey slept through all the noise and fuss.

BILLY   She was the only one who stayed calm.

MRS STEEL   I think it's about time we woke her up, don't you?
They all laugh.

The end

24